SACRED VERSES

PROLOGUE
('WHEN WE WERE YOUNG')
and
PART ONE
(THE JOURNEY BEGINS)

GENE JACKSON

iUniverse, Inc.
Bloomington

SACRED VERSES
PROLOGUE ('WHEN WE WERE YOUNG') and
PART ONE (THE JOURNEY BEGINS)

iUniverse books may be ordered through booksellers or by contacting:

iUniverse
1663 Liberty Drive
Bloomington, IN 47403
www.iuniverse.com
1-800-Authors (1-800-288-4677)

Because of the dynamic nature of the Internet, any web addresses or links contained in this book may have changed since publication and may no longer be valid.

Any people depicted in stock imagery provided by Thinkstock are models, and such images are being used for illustrative purposes only.

Certain stock imagery © Thinkstock.

ISBN: 978-1-4620-0128-6 (sc)
ISBN: 978-1-4620-0129-3 (ebk)

Printed in the United States of America

iUniverse rev. date: 4/12/2011

To Chris:

". . .for he was like, had he been tried,

to have proved most royal."

and, To David,

the Spartan.

Author's Note

The *Divine Comedy* of Dante Aligheiri was written in a strict rhyme scheme of *Terza Rima*. This is feasible in Italian, but is not possible in English. Therefore all of these verses are written in the form of sonnets. By far, the majority are Italian (or Petrarchian), but each chapter ends in one or more Shakespearean sonnets. As far as I am aware this represents the longest sonnet sequence in English literature. The verses are titled as *Sacred,* not in the sense of *Holy* or *Devout,* but following the classical meaning of relating to the spiritual or intellectual universe, instead of the body and the physical world, which would be *Profane.*

"Only to gods in heaven
    Comes no old age or death of anything.
        All else is turmoiled by our master, Time.
            Earth's glory fades,
                And mankind's strength will go away;
Faith dies, and Unfaith blossoms like a flower.
    And who can find, in the open streets of men
        Or secret places of his own heart's love
            One wind blow true forever?"

Sophocles

"Oedipus at Colonnae"

"But soon we too shall die,
    And all memory of those we loved will have left the earth,
        And we ourselves shall be loved for a while and then forgotten.
But the love will have been enough;
    All those impulses of love return to the love that made them.
        Even memory is not necessary for love;

There is a land of the living and a land of the dead,
    And the bridge is love,
        The only survival,
            The only meaning."

T. Wilder

"The Bridge of San Luis Rey"

Volume One
The First Journey

PROLOGUE

WHEN WE WERE YOUNG

When we were young and time was like eternity,
And I believed, as you once used to do,
That to remain both virtuous and true
Was destiny that God reserved for me;
Then I assumed that I would always be
The person that for years I thought I knew,
And that my friends would stay and hold onto
Their membership in our fraternity.
But at the midpoint of my life I found
That I had lost the straight and easy path
That I had followed somewhat thoughtlessly;
When I discovered what in life was sound,
My new awareness and its aftermath
Revealed my former instability.

Now come and sit with me, and I will tell
Of my own journey to enlightenment,
Of fall and rise, of stumbles and ascent,
A pathway that would first descend to hell,
And then, by way of wisdom would dispel
The errant trail of thought, the negligent
Conclusion that prevents the subsequent
Ascension to the holy citadel;
And I would find some stations on the way,
Positions that were halfway in between
Where I could rest and weigh what I had learned.
It was so easy to be led astray,
Because so many things were unforeseen,
And every understanding was hard-earned.

If I believed that I could ever turn
Again into the one I used to be,
I would not speak; nor could I easily
Disclose to you the things I had to learn.
But since I know that no one can return
To innocence and faith once lost, and see
Again a world without complexity,
I'll share with you my newly found concern.
For early in my journey all seemed clear
And faith was simple, life was infinite;
It did not seem essential that I know
Much more than what I saw around me here
Nor could I, at that early time, admit
That much within me I would soon outgrow.

We were, when young, like skaters on a pond,
Delighted with the smooth, new-frozen ice;
Then leaps were confident and turns precise
And skates bit smoothly, forces would respond
With equal opposition, thus the bond
Between the blade and surface would suffice,
Ensuring perfect gliding, and entice
Illusions of tomorrow and beyond.
Our strength was then sufficient to correct
Small errors that arose, adjustments made
Were imperceptible and automatic;
Then any outside force that might affect
Stability was easy to evade,
The future was unbounded and ecstatic.

No one attempted fancy figure-eights
Or patterns that required a smooth precision;
Whoever tried to leap might risk collision
With others in somewhat unsteady states.
Vitality, the strength that animates
A youthful spirit (now beyond my vision)
Is powerful and overwhelms decision
Which, being immature, miscalculates.
For there were dangers that we did not see,
Or, for a while, successfully ignored,
Pretending they were none of our concern.
But even while we skated, glad and free,
The first faint signs appeared and underscored
The agonizing lessons we would learn.

Like skaters in the early morning light,
The time and space before us limitless,
We tried to slip through life without distress,
Avoiding introspection or insight.
Through much of youth it seemed as though we might
Continue on toward constant happiness;
There was no problem we could not finesse,
And nothing that was hidden from our sight.
The sky was always clear, the days were long
And we, with optimistic attitudes
Went blindly on through every endeavor;
So we had confidence that we were strong,
Immune to possible vicissitudes,
And dreamed that life would be this way forever.

But soon the roughened ridges of the ice
Began to multiply and intersect;
With long-continued use and our neglect
And carelessness, they would exact a price.
But only after falling once or twice
Were any of us able to suspect
What none at the beginning could detect:
There was no easy path to paradise.
When twigs and branches from surrounding trees
Begin to fall into the skaters' course,
And interruptions, complications grow
Along with inner doubts and frailties,
Then hesitations start to re-enforce
A less than confident scenario.

So with these changes no one could control,
We skated to the edges, wondering
What might be done that night, if anything,
To clear the imperfections, make it whole
And perfect now. (Although the girasole
Must wait upon the sun, its opening
Depending on the light the day will bring,
We could not tolerate a passive role).
Impatient to continue, and unwise,
Some foolishly went on, imagining
That this perfection could be re-instated;
A little wind to clear the ice, revise
The roughness that was then fore-shadowing
Our future life, but even then, I waited.

THE OLD MAN AND THE SEA

And while I waited there I had a vision;
A man appeared, in youth a paragon
Whose name had meant "the Wise and Honored One".
With genius, riches, health, in competition
He won dramatic prizes; by his admission
Most fortunate of men, he was undone
By age, by failing powers, by a son
Whose motive was not love, but acquisition.
In his old age he was beset by fates
Which no one in his lifespan can avoid,
But not supported by the love, affection
He might expect from family, or mates.
And thus, with honor, pride alone, devoid
Of faith or love, he faced an insurrection.

The old man stood before a hostile sea,
And watched the waves approach, then pause, retreat
And gather strength again, attack his feet
With unrelenting force, tenacity
Unmatched by any human effort he
Had ever seen, or heard, or hoped to meet.
The sucking of its ebb invoked deceit,
The churning flow suggested anarchy.
No wonder he interpreted the ebb
Of ocean's force as equal to his own
Declining strength, and this aggressive flow
To represent the threats, that in a web
So far beyond his power to disown
Would leave him subject to the undertow.

The tide receded, then he turned to me.
"So you have come here, happy, young and strong,
And as with me, your life has gone along
With smooth and easy equanimity.
You must believe me, this is not to be
A situation that you can prolong,
Since fortune will reverse, at last go wrong
And sometimes treat you quite maliciously.
And when this time has come (and it will come),
Your spirit and your heart must be aligned
And ready with a strength that is within you,
A long-established equilibrium.
Then only if your life has been defined
Before your time of need, can you continue."

"And only to the greatest gods will come
No aging, loss, or death of anything;
They live as if in equilibrium,
Immune to sorrow and to sickening.
All else, transfigured by our master, Time,
Will slowly change, and out of life is wrung
The vigor and the strength of mankind's prime,
The beauty and the virtue of the young.
The gods are constant in their love, and when
They do commit themselves, they never tire;
They form a bond that time can not dissever.
But who can find, in open streets of men,
Or secret places of his heart's desire,
A single wind blow constant, true forever?"

"But some will try, there is no harm in trying,
The wonder is how little faith's required
To reassure the sick at heart, the tired,
The lonely souls who spin their lives out crying,
And railing after losses, or denying
That those they trusted, those they most desired
Were not so constant, or were not inspired
Enough to keep that very love from dying.
And those who feel betrayal to be gnawing
Within their very center can be found
Standing with the pebbles on the shore;
For when the tide is at its ebb, withdrawing,
The grating rocks provide a mournful sound,
A melancholy, long, depressive roar."

"And with the best intention, there are those
Who try and fail, but fail to try once more.
One effort, token or sincere, before
They're disappointed in the love they chose.
Then if another episode arose,
Similar to mine along this shore
They would reject, or fearfully ignore
The opportunity that this bestows.
But those who love, and keep their faith alive
Relieve this life's debilitating thirst
For reassurance and serenity.
They gladly from their weariness revive,
And turn again, in fresh relief immersed
As swimmers in the cleanness of the sea."

"But worst are those who do not try at all,
Who simply sit and passively accept
Whatever fate may send, what might befall,
Whose lives are doorsteps, constantly unswept.
For not to know oneself is not to live,
And though there always will be someone greater,
One need not judge himself as negative,
Or lowest general denominator.
Existence which is trapped within despair
And moves as in a fog, without direction
Has neither light, nor love, nor life to share,
Nor peace, nor certitude, nor introspection.
The unexamined life is not worth living;
In this respect the gods are unforgiving."

"But life is very hard to analyze,
It has no solid, finite boundaries,
It is not certain, has no guarantees.
While those outside may surely criticize,
The ones within will always improvise
Illusions to replace realities;
The vigor of our lives, their energies,
Affect our future, static otherwise.
A moving, fluid, changing entity
That will not stop and pose in one position
Nor have a stable or a fixed relation
With other lives, but moves on carelessly,
Is like a picture of an apparition,
A question, but with no good explanation."

Then he was gone, and I of course forgot,
For youth is prone to much procrastination
When life is smooth, without a limitation,
An obstacle, a problem or a knot.
Illusions then, however misbegot
Control our minds, preventing contemplation,
And only later prove an aberration;
We thought we were immortal, we were not.
We knew as little of the world outside
As of the challenges we might expect;
Somehow we thought the innocence of youth
Together with our energy and pride
Would always be sufficient to connect
With universal principles and truth.

Nor did we know ourselves, or how our hearts
Would love, reject, forget or just ignore
Companions, lovers from a time before.
Familiarity or absence starts
To dull the memory, which then departs,
Thus leaving vacancies that heretofore
Were filled with passions nothing can restore;
So who had faith, and all its counterparts,
And what of values on a sacred plane?
Did these exist, and who of us could tell
The valid from the false, expedient,
Which teachings to believe, from which abstain.
And as we circled on life's carousel,
Could we still find a true enlightenment?

And if our minds and spirits saw a light
Illuminating darkness and despair,
Would we have faith and follow anywhere
It seemed to lead us, even though our sight
Could never locate source or satellite?
And what if also we were unaware
Of what, benign or fearsome, waited there,
A mystery with which we would unite?
But at that time we all were immature,
And none of us imagined diminution
Of time unlimited, the mere suggestion
Would certainly have made us insecure.
Not only did we have no good solution,
But no one even dared to ask the question.

For then our youthful naïve innocence
Had perfect faith in firm and compact ice
Which furnished us a harmless paradise
And such a clear and faultless confidence;
For certainly a pure benevolence
Was to be seen, for God would not play dice
With human fate, and never would entice
Someone into a fatal consequence.
But chances happen in our universe,
Perhaps a random, or a destined time
When those who find themselves at some convergence
Of natural events are harmed, or worse.
For life is not a circus pantomime
And no one can rely on God's emergence.

So when a segment of my life dropped out,
With sudden, absolute finality,
Into this open space came fear and doubt
Converting confidence to anarchy.
Then I remembered what the old man taught,
That knowledge of the universe and of one's self,
Of God (or Providence) is not an afterthought,
And wisdom is within, not on the shelf;
No single book contains what life demands,
A painful learning and analysis.
And one more thing the pilgrim understands,
The journey's first and crucial step is this:
As in a maze, to reach the very center,
You first must find the proper place to enter.

Then I was left to find my way alone
Through tangles of a world that had grown cold.
Security had been my cornerstone,
Convictions found in youth, not in the old.
And now I knew at last I must atone
For careless confidence a thousand-fold,
The fault to which the immature are prone,
Without the strength to check or to withhold.
And suddenly within me there had grown
A sense that all of life was less controlled
Than any of my age had ever known;
Experience is always manifold,
The universe was full of questions and
Parameters I could not understand.

THE JOURNEY BEGINS

And thus, about the midpoint of the space
Which I might optimistically expect
To spend on earth, aware of that defect
Which limits time, that also can erase
Illusions of eternity, and trace
A long declining course to intersect
With final states, I started to reflect
On ways to reach a more enlightened place.
The path that I had followed until now
Was easy, plainly marked, through open spaces,
Requiring little effort and no thought
Of where it led, and even less of how
My future might be tied to unknown places
Far different from any I had sought.

But suddenly I found I'd lost my way,
The road no longer seemed as plain or clear,
And unseen obstacles would interfere
With easy progress, leading me astray.
And then I found, with definite dismay
And early feelings of a growing fear
That when familiar landmarks disappear
One's confidence begins to steal away.
My path had ended in a wilderness,
A tangle of a thousand intersections,
All leading in a circle, so that I
Confused and lost, and turning, motionless,
While searching for the cardinal directions
Could not a single one identify.

But just ahead I saw an intersection,
A signpost standing closely by its side;
I thought that with its aid I could decide
Which way to go, if offered a selection
Of routes returning home, or a connection
To easy paths, but this the sign denied.
To my unspoken question, it replied,
"The road of life goes but in one direction."
But then, as if in partial restitution
For canceling my hopes of quick return,
It said that with the courage now to enter
The forest further, part of the solution
Would be provided me, and I would learn
The way to understanding from a mentor.

So I went on, but looking back I saw
The way I'd come already was erased,
A closed forbidding forest had replaced
My path, and this was not the only flaw;
Ahead, a cluttered scene, arousing awe,
For building stones were scattered and displaced
Not showing any order, wildly spaced,
Responsive to no pattern, reason, law.
But in the distance, I could see instead
Of chaos, growing engineering order;
As I went on, the stones, articulating,
Began to form a pavement, and to spread
Into a level terrace, with a border,
And in this space I saw a figure waiting.

In him I found a most unlikely guide,
A twisted form within a metal frame
Who evidently could not walk; this lame
And fragile figure seemed unqualified
To lead me anywhere. He occupied
A prison; in frustration I became
Ungracious, not inquiring of his name,
My attitude an insult to his pride.
He spoke; though difficult to understand,
His attitude was not at all in doubt,
"There are some things, young man, which you forgot.
Appearances deceive and I demand
Respect before I try to help you out.
For you are lost," he said, "and I am not."

He was correct, indeed, I did not know
Where I should go, what I should do; chastised
By my new mentor, I apologized.
And then the situation eased, although
He did not seem the type that would forego
His dominance as teacher. Ill-advised
Mistakes like this had surely jeopardized
The help or guidance that he might bestow.
I called him "Master" out of pure respect,
But he declined the term, he said, because
There was another one that I would meet
Who more deserved the name, the architect
Of many basic principles and laws
Which we in later times would just complete.

"Why have you come," he asked, "along this way
And to this place? And are you serious,
Or merely lost? If you are frivolous
Of purpose, or perhaps a runaway
From boring youth, and wishing to delay
Maturity with endless dubious
Adventures that are only spurious,
Then you could never be my protégé.
But if you are sincere, and wish to learn
The proven truths of life, both old and new,
And will complete the course (you cannot ride
On others' shoulders, here each one must earn
His own reward, and judge his progress too),
Then I will be your mentor. Now decide."

When I considered what this challenge meant
It seemed to represent an intersection
Within my life, at which a new direction
Might now be chosen. Were I confident,
I would agree at once, to give consent
Would lead to long hard work, but on reflection,
The price of grand refusal and rejection
Would be eternal loss and discontent.
And so, I told him that I was aware
Of all the difficulties, but I needed
To know with confidence and not to guess
The basic principles of life and where
I fit into them. For his aid I pleaded:
And "Yes, I will," I said, "I will, oh yes."

Then he replied: "I could explain these things,
The energy, rejection and attraction,
Of subatomic particles, contraction,
Expansion too; I'd show you openings
In galaxies, reveal the colorings
Of stars themselves that undergo refraction,
The speed of light and mass, their interaction,
Dark cavities, loud bangs, and superstrings.
And I could teach you relativity,
Supported by elaborate equations,
Or speak of quantum theory, of whether
One of these should take priority,
Or possibly create by combinations,
A theory of everything, together."

"I could do all of this if you request,
But do not ask too quickly to begin.
You have not gained the needed discipline
And in your naïve state would be hard-pressed
To follow complex theorems, digest
Equations, calculations, that within
Our framework represent the origin
And proof of all the theories expressed.
There will be those who ask you to believe
Fantastic stories, quoting ancient books,
And prophets preaching tales (their own creation),
With stories calculated to deceive,
But all of these, on careful second looks
Will prove to be a mystical evasion."

"You could not understand, without the tools
Of careful research and experience,
Or teachers who have done the work and hence
To separate the wise men from the fools,
The scientific systems from the schools
Of prejudice and superstition whence
Come ignorance. You must at first dispense
With unsubstantiated laws and rules.
So I will send you out to learn, and when
You come again, you will have had a rich
Experience, be also better grounded
In math and calculus and also in
Astronomy, the disciplines on which
Our knowledge of the universe is founded."

"But do not be discouraged or distressed;
You are not truly lost if you're aware
Of what you need to find. Do not compare
A seeker like yourself who has expressed
Desire for wisdom with the dispossessed,
Who in their mindless comfort cannot bear
To rouse themselves from sleep, or do not care,
A fine first step is ignorance confessed.
So children waking from their infancy
First find themselves and wonder who they are,
And how they came to be, and also where
Their lives might lead, and how to find the key
To existential themes, all very far
From anything of which they'd been aware."

So he had indicated I should go
Along a certain road without delay,
"Your journey will be long, a tiresome way
And often progress will be very slow.
But if you pay attention, even though
The lessons may be difficult today,
Tomorrow's gain will certainly repay
Your energy, with all you need to know."
But I had one more question, while departing,
"It seems that all around me is surreal,
And yet I still have faith that there must be
A plan for all. So why are you imparting
Directions, pathways, what they might reveal,
Why are you here? Who sent you here to me?"

He said, "We are not personalities,
But essences, distilled from prior lives,
And can be called back from our present ease
To intervention, thus the soul survives
Beyond the time that it is linked to earth.
And if we can contribute and provide
Our wisdom to the living, it is worth
A major effort, we are satisfied.
I felt a strong compulsion and I came;
Who summoned me, I truly cannot tell.
Though spirits seldom keep a private name,
It must be someone who had loved you well.
For love can penetrate, as with a knife
The curtain separating death from life."

There in his words I felt a latent hint
Of something unexpressed, yet indirect
And almost semi-hidden, circumspect
As if he were a little diffident,
Reluctant to express his real intent.
However, I was able to detect
Enough between his words; I could connect
The inference of what he truly meant:
There is a power in the universe
Mysterious and nebulous, pervasive
Throughout the future and the past combined
That should at times be able to coerce;
At least with spirits it would be persuasive,
This was the force, the essence I must find.

He turned away, already having shown
Me much of this initial episode
Of my enlightenment. He had bestowed
A challenge that began with one unknown.
I looked back when I reached a marker stone,
But he was gone, the one to whom I owed
So much could not come with me on the road;
Without my guide, then, I went on alone.
I was unsure of what I might expect,
How far ahead to look, who might appear,
(And whether, learning, I would be the worst
Of students); would there be an architect,
A poet, prophet, artist, engineer?
I only knew the Greeks should be the first.

THE MAN WHO COUNTED NUMBERS

My mentor left without another word
Across the terrace paved with fitted stones,
Committing me to multiple unknowns;
For as I thought of all that I had heard,
Articulated and what he inferred,
I knew this was the time when one disowns
The superficial years of life, atones
For all the senseless acts that had occurred.
He had assigned a lengthy regimen
That must commence before I thought of sleep;
My unexamined life was disappearing,
A new one beckoned as I took again
The pathway through the forest, close and deep,
Until at last it ended in a clearing.

And there I saw a man who stood alone,
While drawing complex figures on the ground.
A few of them were angled, some were round,
And some attempted depth, a sphere, a cone.
Beside them were equations, symbols known
Or quite imaginary; with profound
Intensity of thought, without a sound
He traced the figures that were all his own.
There was no conversation when I moved
Much closer to observe his calculations;
He took me for a student, and explained
His theories, and asked if I approved.
He demonstrated figures and equations,
The abstract corollaries they contained.

I asked his name and what he sought to find.
"Truth in numbers, using them to reach
A system, based in logic, in which each
New theory is tested and defined,
Thus leading toward a discipline of mind.
I try to think of principles, and teach
An ordered thought and clarity of speech
In which the steps to wisdom are combined.
My name? Pythagoras the traveler,
Who saw Egyptians counting cows and grain,
And Persians counting soldiers. But to me,
The geometric forms of cylinder
And pyramid and temple square contain
The secrets solving their complexity."

"I found that mathematics was the key
And took these numbers out of common use;
Their abstract force allowed me to deduce
The laws that govern plane geometry.
I proved an always constant sum of three
Angles, whether right, acute, obtuse,
That sides, compared to their hypotenuse
Were governed by equations, rigidly.
Beyond these numbers logic, still expanding,
Might unify the laws of life, and our
New axioms, once proven, bring diverse
Events into good order. Understanding,
Promoted to a universal power,
Could govern all this world and universe."

"It could, indeed, define all stars and space
Or as I called it, 'kosmos', meaning all
Contained within the universe, the small
Invisible, as well as commonplace
Constituents of life that interface
With greater forces still; these always fall
Within eternal rules that gods install
And men discover, but cannot erase.
As numbers can be factored down to prime,
All life can be reduced to simple laws.
The total universe which, centered here
On earth, if it obeys this paradigm,
Would then be proven perfect, without flaws,
A regulated, pulsing, living sphere."

He did not recognize his limitations,
And though he had discovered two dimensions
And drawn and graphed them well, still his foundations
Must wait on others' work for their extensions.
For though he thought the universe a sphere
His figures and geometry were flat.
The depth of solid spaces stayed unclear
(Then later Euclid formulated that);
And even then, their universe was static,
Allowing neither time nor change of speed,
Till Isaac Newton found that mathematic
Laws of time and gravity agreed.
With all this still to come, I left him there,
Considering a circle in a square.

THE ANCIENT ENGINEER

But I continued on; to my surprise,
Along the way, I saw some groups of men
Some distance from my road. I thought that when
I came this way again I'd improvise
A conversation, now it seemed unwise;
And I went further, until once again,
I saw ahead a novel group, and then
Approached to see whom I could recognize.
Attendants stood with towels close around
A giant tub that, filled up to the rim,
Was set across the center of my path,
Therein a man so low he might have drowned.
One servant, speaking, indicated him,
"Do not disturb the Master in his bath."

Then he went on: "Nor is it also wise
To stand between our Master and the sun.
He loves the warmth, and still remembers one
Astounding and unfortunate surprise,
And if alarmed might sink and moisturize
Your feet." Confused, I thought I was undone,
Until the servants said in unison,
"Come close, he will converse and not baptize."
So, gingerly I then approached the tub
And took a spot where servants once had been,
And waited for a proper introduction,
Which never came. They wanted me to scrub
Their Master's back. I did, and trapped within
This comic state, I waited for instruction.

Then, still within the tub, he stood upright,
And pointed out how much the water fell,
And sat back down, intending to compel
It once again to rise. Its final height
Then should be as before, this time, not quite.
His rapid downward movement did propel
A wave outside the tub, which sloshed and fell
Upon my feet, for which he was contrite.
In consequence, he asked me to sit down
And learn the state of science at his time,
And how he saw the universe to be.
Indifferent to any robe or gown,
Quite stiffly he himself began to climb
Out of his bath, to sit down next to me.

I asked about the groups that I had seen
Along the way, and what they might discuss.
"Philosophers, and all quite garrulous,"
He said, "debating arguments between
Their own ideas and principles; they glean
The leavings of the scientists like us
But do not know an arc from radius,
Or average from median or mean.
There are Lyceums and Academies
That argue endlessly, but never move
Past abstract concepts, whether small or greater.
They specialize in vague hypotheses
Which they imagine well, but never prove;
You will encounter their confusion later."

"But you have come to me to learn, by science
The proven nature of reality;
And this is very well, as you will see.
For those who serve our discipline are clients
Uniquely of objective truth; compliance
Is still reserved for tests, done honestly
With clear results, that mathematically
Are logical, and merit our reliance.
There is no vague and useless speculation
Permitted in the scope of science, nor
Is any system seemingly invested
For benefit or gain. The revelation
Of priest or prophet we alike abhor,
As with our own hypotheses, untested."

"But as my recent and complete immersion
Should prove to you, if you have thought it through,
The water level fell as I withdrew
And rose to overflow on my submersion.
On careful measuring of this conversion
Of human volume under water to
The volume spilled outside the tub, then you
Can make a universal, true assertion:
The body that is floating or submerged
Is less in weight (or else it would not float).
Its size, determined by empirical
Assessment, equals water that emerged.
When put into a formula I wrote
They called it "Archimedes' principle.""

"And please do not confuse this with my Screw,
For this is nothing like imagination
Might well suppose; Egyptian irrigation
Required the raising of the water through
Successive altitudes, what I could do
Was merely to improve acceleration.
When farmers used this minor adaptation
They gave me much more credit than was due.
The 'Principle' was something else again;
It was a stroke of genius, I might say
Myself (I think that others would agree),
And warranted my celebration, when
I ran through streets in famous disarray
On measuring specific gravity."

"When I was young, I loved the physical
Equipment which I used to demonstrate
The ways in which a large and heavy weight
Was easily propelled with minimal
Duress, applied with geometrical
Advantage. Building many intricate
Designs, then I could still anticipate
That I might need to sway the skeptical.
So I proposed a quite unique endeavor:
A system that I would construct on land
And pull a mighty warship to her berth
With ropes and pulleys, and perhaps a lever.
Give me a fulcrum, and a place to stand,
And I believe that I could move the earth."

"The king of Syracuse (upon this boast),
Had challenged me to demonstrate, first-hand,
By pulling his great royal ship, full-manned
Up from the ocean, beach it on the coast.
Devising pulleys, building up almost
To infinite the force at my command,
The ship attached by cable to the land,
I drew it by my efforts to the post.
But here, I think, is quite a paradox;
For all of these observers, when they see
The movement of a vessel as it floats
Will feel I moved the ship onto the docks,
Not thinking of the possibility:
I may have moved the earth out to the boats."

He was a military engineer
Who ranked among the finest of his age,
And with his grasp of force and leverage
Designed great catapults, and other gear.
All these could hurl a heavy stone or sphere
With great precision he alone could gauge,
Attacking ships at sea or anchorage,
The ancient world's outstanding cannoneer.
He hated war and chaos; clarity
Would give his private spirit pure delight.
To him, his missiles' highest watermark
Lay in their intricate geometry,
The beauty of projectiles while in flight,
Their long and lovely parabolic arc.

"Young man", he said, "I think you are correct,
For as you see, I'm really not aggressive
Except in conversation. I'm obsessive
There, and in my writing, circumspect
In every other possible respect.
And those who find my verbiage excessive
Admit my clarity to be impressive,
The marker of a first-class intellect.
Now, you would like for me to summarize
The efforts that I think significant
Before you leave to go along your path.
I'll tell you things I think epitomize
My work, but only the most relevant,
And then, once more, I will enjoy my bath."

"I squared the circle, calculated *pi* ,
Advanced geometry and mathematics,
Proposed the formulas to verify
The areas of spirals and quadratics.
And I protected Syracuse, my home,
With land defenses, and amphibian,
And checked invading forces sent from Rome,
'Purely by the genius of one man.'
I found that logarithms could express
A number that is far too great to measure,
And one infinitesimal, or less.
I did these things, but for my greatest pleasure,
I looked into the heavens; nothing mars
The beauty of the Law that moves the stars."

THE MAN WHO LOOKED
AT THE STARS

Then I went on, and soon the trees enclosed
The path again; the forest now seemed dark,
As far as I could see ahead. The stark
Oppressive outlook here was unopposed
By any light; as prejudice in closed
And rigid minds perpetuates an arc
Descending into ignorance, the mark
Of knowledge not discovered, but imposed.
The time seemed endless, centuries or more,
But this was surely wrong, for time can be
Both absolute and relative; what could
Be measured with precision long before
Now often seems to us, subjectively,
Both shorter, and much longer than it should.

So I continued on with little rest
Up to an open place, while slowly night
Had come. Across the field I had the sight
Of two men standing there almost abreast,
And peering to the sky as if obsessed
Through tapered tubes at distant, speckled light,
Their concentration such I thought they might
Ignore completely that they had a guest.
But then the nearer turned to look at me,
So I could see the wonder on his face;
An introduction seemed obligatory,
And so I asked him what he sought to see
While looking at a vast and empty space,
"God's Heaven itself," he said, "In all its glory."

He let me look into his "telescope";
"Primitive", he said, "but what I see
Reveals a universe that holds the key
To understanding who we are, the hope
Of finding truth. You see the envelope
Of space and motion here, within must be
The secrets of the world, its destiny;
I only wish that you might be the Pope.
For I would show him proof, as I'll show you,
Phenomena that prove without a doubt
A system of the planets that esteemed
Philosophers like Aristotle (who
Though not a Christian, yet could serve devout
Ecclesiastic purpose) never dreamed."

His name was Nicholas Copernicus,
Or so had been five hundred years ago,
And whether Pole or German (who could know?)
His education was Italian, thus
He was exposed to Greeks; Aristarchus
(Two thousand years before) had tried to show
The earth to move around the sun, although
He could not prove what he thought obvious.
And then, two hundred Anno Domini,
One, Ptolemy of Alexandria,
Pre-empted for a thousand years the scheme,
Insisting strongly that the earth must be
The center of the stars, and this idea
Left Biblical theology supreme.

Much later, honest questions had begun
Occurring here and there; da Vinci taught:
"The sun itself moves not. The earth is not
The center of the circle of the sun
Nor centered in the universe", but one
Of many minor planets God forgot
Until development of human thought
Reversed its course into oblivion.
But no one had a true analysis
Or proof until Copernicus, with mental
Skills, but instruments of little worth,
Computed orbits of the spheres; while this
(His mathematic work) was elemental,
Still, with these basic tools, he moved the earth.

He said he had observed and calculated
Positions and the courses of the spheres.
"And each celestial galaxy appears
To have its center." This accommodated
His model of the earth and moon, which stated:
"Each satellite and circling moon adheres
Within an orbit which is fixed for years
Around a focus, which is designated.
But each is single, none will overlap
With any other galaxy, nor any
Center duplicate another. Seek
Throughout the sky, and you will find the map
Of all the heavens is diverse, with many
Far-separated systems, each unique."

"The motions of the Earth in part explain
The movement of the planets, both direct
And retrograde, which often we detect
And wonder why they frequently contain
Apparent inequalities. The strain
Of what we see against what we expect
Can be resolved by knowing the effect
And error moving platforms can sustain.
The highest heaven never changes, while
The earth itself performs a full rotation
Around its central axis once a day.
This changed perspective thus can reconcile
Apparent movement of the stars, migration
Across the sky presents a false display."

He thought the center of the earth to be
The point toward which our circling moon's rotation
Was always fixed, and also the location
And central focus of our gravity.
But, calculating distance carefully,
From earth to moon and sun, and estimation
Of mass and weight of each, his explanation
Of all these facts showed simple clarity:
The earth was not the center of the sun
And its rotation, but a satellite,
A minor one at that. And in one stroke
The work of Aristotle was undone,
Theology itself no longer right,
And minds asleep a thousand years awoke.

The orbits of the planets he observed
Revolved around the sun, consistently.
And more than this, each course he could foresee
Would follow such a path that always curved
Around a central solar point; this served
To unify his central theory:
That all the spheres and planets, properly,
Would occupy the planes that they reserved.
The planes were static, but the planets moved,
Along an endless path that, he had found,
Would center and conserve, but not disperse,
Its force of gravity. And thus he proved,
The earth, like all the planets, moved around
The sun, the center of the universe.

He measured by geometry at night
The canopy of stars, the firmament,
Compared this number with the subsequent
Computed distance to the sun, the height
And ratio almost infinite; despite
The indirectness of his measurement,
He found it greater than the evident
Diameter of earth, and he was right.
From these comparisons came this conclusion:
Our size, and that of earth, and of the spheres,
Is imperceptible against the whole
Entirety, dispelling the delusion
Of our importance, substituting fears
Beyond our comprehension or control.

He demonstrated planets in their spheres
And showed that they must rotate, with the sun
As central to their orbit, and that one
Important to us all, the earth, adheres
To rules that govern others, and appears
To also move in orbit; thus begun,
His study of a new phenomenon
Would lead to others, stirring ancient fears.
And so his Commentaries brought reaction
From those invested in the rigid past;
And those who could not tolerate the facts
Demanded the immediate retraction
Of all the evidence he had amassed,
And threatened persecution for his acts.

The problem for theology was this:
That if the universe were infinite,
And earth so minor, why would God permit
His law, His Son, His entire edifice
To start and flourish here? If genesis
Of universal forces could omit
A central role for earth and men, then it
Must be declared a false hypothesis.
Alarmed their God might not be universal,
They kept Him as a captive of their bias,
Concerned with human actions as befits
A chosen people; this enforced reversal
Was led by those fanatical and pious
Defenders of the faith, the Jesuits.

The Church itself raised only mild objection
To his hypothesis; the Inquisition
However, took a firm and strict position.
Giordano Bruno added his projection
From theory to fact, and its correction
Was swift and violent; their opposition
Was to Copernicus in recognition
Of danger of religious redirection.
The forms of retribution ranged from small
Brief censorship to burning at the stake,
And *heresy* for those agreeing with
This edifice, in order to forestall
The hidden dangers that might now unmake
The lovely poetry of Christian myth.

Then he was old, and all his work reviled
By Calvin and by Luther, with the hope
That Scripture would prevail; unreconciled,
He gained the brief approval of the Pope.
But then the Church itself turned to the past,
Declaring him to be a heretic.
His peers paid scant attention, so at last
He went away, dejected and heart-sick.
His structure fell, unnoticed there until
Another generation could replace
Established prejudice with truth, but still
It marked an effort no one could erase.
And sometimes, too, was seen against the sky,
A single column, still too proud to die.

THE MAN WHO MADE THE EARTH MOVE

I looked toward him once more, but he was gone;
He faded silently, as in the past,
Until the others came, who all surpassed
His pioneering work. So I moved on,
Pursuing constantly the paragon
Of wisdom that my mentor had forecast.
This man, almost the first, was not the last,
There would be others in the pantheon,
And one of these was standing very near.
He had a larger, grander telescope,
His own design, and did not hesitate,
Inviting me to look. He did appear
(To judge the contents by the envelope)
The essence of a genius incarnate.

When he looked up from study, and I saw
His countenance, the forehead, piercing eyes,
And noble face, I did apologize
For being not his equal, but a raw
Untutored seeker, with a major flaw,
One that I hoped he would not criticize.
And in his presence I could not disguise
My feeling: total, overwhelming awe.
"I never met a man so ignorant
I could not learn some valid things from him,"
He said to me; then, "But I do admit
That sometimes prejudice or arrogant
Apostles of stupidity can trim
My peacefulness and self-control a bit."

He had no trouble with diversity
For "gladly would he learn and gladly teach,"
And never in his life was known to preach
A doctrine based in un-reality.
But there were times in which serenity
Was tested, as when someone would impeach
His motives, then civility would reach
A limit, nearly to catastrophe.
He could not tolerate a hypocrite
And thought a papal bull abomination,
And all of history recalls the famous
Encounter with a pious Jesuit
Defending Ptolomy; with indignation,
He called him "eunuch, fool, and ignoramus".

Much like a child in school, he loved to play
With things he could construct and modify,
But with this difference: to clarify
The principles these structures would display.
Thus pulleys, levers, inclines, this array
Became the pathway to identify
Dynamic principles that quantify
The laws of physics that they all obey.
He built a special broken inclined plane,
So he could roll a polished ball, a sphere
Along (and down) one leg and up another.
Then measuring the height it could attain,
(Discounting friction which might interfere),
The first and final heights should match each other.

"The static and dynamic principles
That govern mass and matter, their existence,
Their motion (with a frictional resistance
Like atmosphere, which changes or annuls
The speed of matter, spheres and particles),
Allow them to advance a certain distance
Affected constantly by the persistence
Of gravity and other obstacles.
But mass itself can never disappear,
But only is transformed, and not destroyed.
And since it will appear as energy
Upon its transformation, it is clear
That there is no such concept as a void
On earth, in heaven, or a galaxy."

"But many times solutions seem to lead
To new associated problems; so
It was that day at Pisa, even though
I proved unequal weights had equal speed
When falling freely. All who watched agreed,
The rate of fall for both at first was slow,
But faster as they neared the ground below,
Until they fell quite rapidly, indeed.
I saw the problem of increasing rates,
And wondered if the change was linear,
And if it reached a limit, a plateau.
But now I see that this anticipates
A novel discipline, quite singular,
The calculus, whose rules I did not know."

Dividing properties of mass into
Essential parts, he felt that one perspective
Would be: that all that could be called objective
And dealt with mathematically are true
And lasting properties of objects, due
To their inherent being, while subjective
Sensations such as sound were ineffective
Without the presence of an outside view.
Thus density and motion and position
Are constant and unique and permanent,
Intrinsic to the body, not created.
But qualities existing on condition
Of sensory effects are different,
And fleeting, and can be eliminated.

He read the works of Aristotle first,
(Philosophers accepted them outright,
And learned theologians, erudite,
And pious in conformity immersed
Themselves in orthodoxy and coerced
All others to believe the same, despite
The total lack of proof that they were right).
But in *his* case, conviction was reversed.
Distrusting abstract thought that was not grounded
In demonstration and experiment,
He knew that he could prove without a doubt
That ancient doctrines never had been founded
On any solid base, but that dissent
Would be opposed by all who were devout.

"Just one example, easy to recall,
A firm experiment, and not a guess;
For it is easy, out of carelessness
To make up stories with no proof at all.
So, Aristotle taught that if a ball
Of greater mass was dropped with one of less,
That, strictly due to greater heaviness,
The large one would fall faster than the small.
But I found weights that were two different sizes,
And dropped them from a certain leaning height.
(Philosophers and students refereed
To cancel any bias or surprises).
They struck the ground as one, to my delight,
Because they traveled at an equal speed."

He carefully assessed the views proposed
A hundred years before, and since rejected
By many theologians, well-respected;
For all of them were equally disposed
To blindly follow doctrine, and with closed
Conforming minds, relied upon selected
Quotations from the Scriptures, which detected
Grave heresy for views which they opposed.
And now, when faced with danger once again,
This intersection of our history
Was crucial; on this singular decision
Would hinge the future of our world: sustain
The errors of the past, conformity,
Or open to a new and honest vision.

And then he read the book Copernicus
Had written over eighty years before,
And found a logic he could not ignore;
But very few were willing to discuss
Proposals so heretical, and thus
He quietly continued to explore,
Collecting proofs, attempting to restore
A system that to him was obvious.
He did have allies, some of whom he taught,
And some like Kepler, equals, genuine
Associates, with whom he could relate,
And there were several others; still he thought
The ranks of honest intellects were thin,
The number of the asinine was great.

He felt that better lenses would permit
Advanced discoveries that none had known
Or found before, and to this cornerstone
Of vision in the sky he would commit.
When first he could not find the requisite
Design of frame and lens, he made his own.
His very first crude instrument alone
Enlarged an image only by a bit.
But with this telescope he saw a new
Expanse of stars that never had been seen.
The surface of the moon had heretofore
Been specified as smooth, but now he knew
That it had mountains, valleys in between;
And there were other thousands to explore.

And with the power of this instrument
He saw the moons that circle Jupiter,
And postulated things that might occur.
With phases of the planets evident,
As they would travel past the sun, this meant
Their changes of illumination were
A proof the sun is central, and infer
The basic structure of the firmament.
Then he improved his telescope until
It magnified the stars a thousand times,
And he could see much deeper into space.
These observations now began to fill
Essential roles in forming paradigms
That would the ancient ignorance replace.

He published "Two chief systems of the World,
The Ptolemaic and Copernican",
And then at once the Inquisition hurled
Their charges of a greater danger than
The Calvinists and Lutherans. Their four
"Examinations" led to the retraction
Of his beliefs; he said he would restore
The earth to central motionless inaction.
And so, humiliated, tired and old,
He seemed defeated, forced at last to utter
Apologies for truth, and to uphold
"Correct" belief. But he was heard to mutter:
"No matter what you think your Scripture proves,
Regardless of your doctrine, still, it moves."

A MIND UNEQUALED AND INFINITE

As I went on my way, I found that night
Had faded while I peered into the sky;
The stars had gently gone, the moon was high
But pale against the growing eastern light.
Then in a pleasant field I saw in flight
And darting here and there a dragonfly,
That hovered in advance to signify
That somewhere up ahead he would alight.
He led me to an orchard and a hedge
And rested in the sheltered garden there,
So coming close behind, I saw that he
Was offering to me this privilege:
To meet a rumpled man, who in a chair
Was sitting at his ease beneath a tree.

The dragonfly had settled on his hat,
But this he did not notice, concentrating
On distant abstract questions. I stood waiting,
Unwilling to disturb him as he sat
And thought through mathematic problems that
Consistently engaged his mind, creating
An awkward pause. While I was hesitating,
An apple fell from tree to ground, ker-splat.
This brought him back into reality
And he stood up, a little agitated
To realize that he was not alone.
Then he apologized, on seeing me,
"I knew that you were coming, while I waited,
I drifted into spaces all my own."

"And when I am alone, I seldom sit
But much prefer to stroll or walk about.
If you will come with me and go throughout
These garden paths, and if you will permit
Unique instruction, you will benefit."
I told him there was certainly no doubt
That I would listen patiently without
Complaint; my profit would be infinite.
"You will be welcome, but I'm sure you know
That years ago, I taught at Trinity
And of my students there, a very few
Would come to class a second time, although
Not one could understand consistently
When I would try to teach them what I knew."

Then he took off his hat, his hair was thatched,
(The dragonfly flew off) and I could see
That he was under-dressed, quite carelessly;
His necktie was undone, his coat was patched,
And looking down, his stockings were unmatched,
His shoes were old, and worn as they could be.
Then vaguely, almost absent-mindedly,
He stopped and asked me, seemingly detached:
"Young man, again please tell me who you are."
"A student, sir," I said, "for your instruction,
A pilgrim, making progress, so I hope,
And I have come through time and space so far,
To seek a scientific introduction
To wisdom of the very broadest scope."

We set out walking, then he stopped once more,
"I need to know if you have heard the story
Which I consider just an allegory,
(And rather silly, too) that I deplore.
But still, its one I never can ignore
Since everyone believes that *a priori*
It must be true, and thus a purgatory
Awaits me if you've heard the tale before."
He meant the apple falling on his head,
Which first of all would represent bad luck,
And second was undignified, and third,
"The whole thing was ridiculous," he said,
"For who could think at all, on being struck
By falling missiles from a tree or bird?"

I sensed that he was very sensitive
About the legend, therefore I assured
Him that I'd never heard it, then detoured
Around the subject from then on, to give
Him room and space to move to substantive
Profound ideas which could have been obscured
By trivia; and with my place secured,
I asked him to resume his narrative.
"But you must understand, I watched it fall,
It landed at my feet, I saw it there,
And studied it at length, for it was worth
A fortune, proof of forces drawing all
Our bodies, also objects everywhere
Directly toward the center of the earth."

We walked around his garden in the sun,
He would, on every circuit, expedite
My education, and with great insight
Explain a difficult phenomenon.
We circled, more or less in unison,
He, being like an ancient anchorite
Emerging with an eager acolyte
Expanded on the lesson he'd begun.
And as we walked along the garden path,
He lectured me concerning many things
I barely fathomed in the interim
But might remember in the aftermath.
So, filtered through the fog that distance brings,
These were the lessons I absorbed from him.

The passion of his life was to explain
The key to natural philosophy
By mathematics, with its brevity
And accurate descriptions, which attain
Concise and balanced form, and which abstain
From guesswork and from speculation, free
Of prejudice; he searched for facts, to see
The basic principles that they sustain.
He was a compound of imagination
And mathematic rigor, hazarding
No speculation in advance, but testing
With his experiments and computation
A group of difficult and challenging
Hypotheses which I found interesting.

He conjured up in his imagination
Some particles of matter lying near
To one another (none that would adhere),
And thought about their mutual relation.
Now would there be an infinite stagnation?
A situation where they would appear
To have no influence or interfere
With one another's site or situation?
Perhaps they'd wander off to unplanned places,
Rejecting one another randomly,
Forever fated to remain alone;
Or would they cover intervening spaces
To crash together, with the property
Of penetrating one another's zone?

Whichever of these systems might be true,
Indifference, repulsion or attraction,
Expansion of the volume or contraction,
Or simply "status quo", one thing he knew:
The answer would be found conforming to
A principle, which to the satisfaction
Of mathematic law, not to abstraction,
Could be expressed so none could misconstrue.
For this to work, he needed an equation
That must include the masses, all their sizes
Expressed as weight; an element involved
That must be given much consideration
Is distance, and the force that it comprises
Is inverse, as the balance is resolved.

To balance his equation, first he needed
To settle his hypothesis, which way
Would particles relate? And so that day
He saw the object fall, and then proceeded
To think about the action, which he heeded
As no one had. The bodies which obey
The laws of mutual attraction lay
Intrinsic to the way that he succeeded.
For later he would say the key was that
The problem he considered without ceasing
Could be explained and solved by principles
Which he called "Laws of Motion". This format
Is central to our physics, both increasing
Our knowledge and removing obstacles.

One barrier remained, he must define
The way that distance altered the co-action
Of bodies in a mutual attraction.
A greater space between would undermine
Attractive force, but how could he consign
A value more specific than abstraction?
For all could see that it would be a fraction;
This inverse numeral he must refine.
First, based on Kepler's findings, several
Had clarified the law of inverse squares.
But he alone confirmed by calculation:
For bodies, linked in space, the integral
Attraction grew with masses of the pairs
Diminished by the square of separation.

The tree he sat beneath (before the fall),
Extended one long arm beyond his chair,
A lovely arc descending through the air,
And curving toward the ground, elliptical,
End-weighted with a smooth and spherical
Firm object on the very tip, and there
It hung straight down, suspended in mid-air,
A balance of two forces, vertical.
"For every action there will always be
A second equal energy, opposing
The vector of the first;" resultant tension
Is always balanced if stability
Is present in the system, pre-supposing
An equilibrium in each dimension.

"An unattended mass can be at rest,"
(And certainly the apple seemed to be),
"And will continue in serenity,
Unless external forces manifest
A total change." And this could be expressed
By raising of the pressure that we see,
Or by release of tense stability;
So, either way, the balance would be stressed.
And as he watched, the small attachment broke,
The branch, released, became upright again,
And quivered, as it tried to overcome
The liberation and the counterstroke,
Establishing a stable setting then
With new, distinctive equilibrium.

"An unattended mass can also be
In motion, uniform and straight," and thus,
The apple fell without ambiguous
Coincidence, but with conformity
To preordained direction, and was free
Of deviation or circuitous
Meanderings. It fell, precipitous,
Direct and straight, and with alacrity.
It struck the ground, he saw, some feet away,
While having deviated not one bit,
Not one degree or centimeter wide
Of its predicted line, because its way
Was never changed by any definite
Or minor force that could be verified.

But what "predicted line" would be correct?
The answer lay in his imagination,
For he could see the apple's destination
Continuing the line which would bisect
The earth, straight to its center, then project
On outwards to the point of liberation,
The static apple's center; observation
Confirmed exactly what he did expect.
So, now he had two masses, one was small,
And one was very large, but their attraction
Was mutual, and could not be denied.
Their separation known, the integral
Components of the calculated action
Were present, all had been identified.

The change that is produced by alteration
Of any body, static (or "at rest")
Or moving in a certain line is best
Described as relative attenuation,
(Perhaps with equal truth, as augmentation
Depending on the motive force impressed).
The second to the first is always stressed,
According to its strength and angulation.
If for their pathways vectors are devised
The two will meet and merge, a new direction
Distinct from both the second and the first
May be revealed, the vectors, analyzed,
Can indicate how far this new deflection
Will cause the path to change, or be reversed.

Thus gravity, related to the square
Of distance separating any two
Such bodies in the universe, outgrew
Its old conception, now that any pair
No matter what their mass, and anywhere
They might be placed by chance, would have a true
Attraction to each other, and accrue
A weight that just the two of them would share.
But all the planets, all the stars were thus
Within the law of mutual attraction,
Each felt a pull from every other source.
The sum of gravities, the impetus
And energy from all was no abstraction,
But was a balance and a complex force.

For there must be a pressure, opposition
Against the inward pull that so attracts
The stars throughout the sky, and counteracts
The rule of gravity, so this condition
Exactly balances, by definition.
Each one of two opposing strengths impacts
The planets equally, and so protracts
Their orbits; each can hold its own position.
The force opposing had been calculated
By Halley and by Kepler in the past,
To satisfy observed relationships
Between the planets and their centers, stated
This way: their planetary laws forecast
Each orbit in the shape of an ellipse.

But though he formulated many laws
And proved the principles of gravity,
And though he calculated carefully,
Avoiding and correcting any flaws,
The zealots still objected, some because
His space and time and motion seemed to be
Conclusive, standing independently
Without the need of God or Primal Cause.
He tried as best he could to make amends,
By saying that the system of the sun
And stars and planets was unique, so odd,
And yet consistent, that its cause transcends
Its mechanism. Yet, when all was done,
"It still remains mysterious as God".

But neither could he offer explanation
Of how, exactly, gravity could act
Through miles of empty space and still attract
And alter other masses, gravitation
Might still be magical, like levitation.
But when he saw his theory attacked,
Despite its mathematic and exact
Support, he did not hide this limitation.
He then confessed at once: he did not know
If there might be an agent for transmission;
Would it be real or immaterial?
Would it be static, or perhaps might flow
Throughout the ether? His sincere admission
Was honest, true and not equivocal.

At last I was exhausted, even then,
He showed no sign that he was even slowing.
As I became lethargic, he was growing
In energy, activity, and when
I went to sleep, he asked if oxygen
Might possibly revive me for ongoing
Discussion, for the prior to-and-fro-ing
He wanted to experience again.
I felt however, I had heard enough;
As at a banquet, one must not abuse
Abundance, or be overwhelmed. I knew
My finite brain contained what he could stuff
Therein, but could not tolerate profuse
Material my mind could not work through.

And so, he left me there, asleep at last,
To dream of shining visions I had seen,
That his (and others') prophecies forecast,
And esoteric concepts made routine.
He went on walking, thinking, quite alone,
Unable now to find a stable place
On which his mind could rest, for he was prone
To manic thoughts which he could not erase.
I had discovered my own limitation;
He showed, in contrast, just the opposite,
In reasoning and in imagination
His aptitude seemed almost infinite.
I knew with certainty I'd never find
In all my wanderings, an equal mind.

THE KINDLY UNCLE

I was so tired, I might have slept for years,
But woke at last to find a famous face
I recognized at once, who watched the space
Where I lay sleeping, as one volunteers
At vigils or at wakes; one who appears
Attentive, yet detached, alert in case
The honored guest should stir, and so erase
The rationale for sadness in his peers.
But I, awaking, was at first confused,
I felt reality to be suspended;
For it was not until I saw his pipe,
And smelled it too (he seemed to be amused),
That I then realized and comprehended
Eccentric genius, and its prototype.

He seemed to be a kindly man, and gentle,
And rather like an uncle that you knew
In early childhood, but who turned into
A vague eccentric; by some accidental
Affair he went away, or by parental
Estrangement from his family withdrew,
Was lost for years, and now quite well-to-do,
Returned with wealth and fame, both monumental.
He seemed somewhat bewildered at his luck,
Or genius, or achievement, what you will,
Yet somewhat pleased, amused at all the fuss
That strangers made of him, for he was stuck
With constant obligations to fulfill,
The fantasies of all the envious.

He wore a loose and somewhat floppy sweater,
And looked as if that was his formal suit;
His comfort as he was, was absolute,
For he was neither creditor, no debtor.
And for his confidence there were (still better),
Two talents that together constitute
The greatest academic attribute:
His memory, and also his "forgetter".
Because of this, he always concentrated
On problems with an open mind, uncluttered
By any useless knowledge from the past;
This mental open space accommodated
A resting place for thoughts that might have fluttered
Far out into the ether, lost, outcast.

"Good morning, you are here to find out why
The famous 'e' that equals 'm-c²' ,
Is so immense, and famous everywhere;
You want to find out how it is that I,
A lowly patent clerk could prophesy
That energy and mass together share
Their interchanging properties, declare
That mass will change as forces multiply.
How could I alter Newton's universe
That stood so static for three hundred years,
And say that beams of light can move in curves,
That space and time are relative, and worse,
The speed of light is not what it appears,
Unlike the speed of objects one observes?"

"I was instructed to enlighten you
On principles of relativity
(Both general and special) that would be
A useful basis for transition to
A modern system. But so very few
Can understand its deep complexity
That I propose, in all humility,
To offer just a simple over- view.
But first, about that job as patent clerk,
(Probationary, technical, third class),
It offered vacant space I used in linking
My thoughts and proofs; and not requiring work
(Although one might regret the rank, alas),
It left a lot of time for abstract thinking."

And he was quite correct, I never could
Have followed any detailed explanations
Or comprehended multiple equations
That few within this world had understood.
And so we made a bargain, that he would
Provide me with some general summations,
Abstaining from the worst of complications
That would arise somehow, in likelihood.
And on my part, I'd try to pay attention,
And never interrupt or make suggestions.
He said that there were only two or three
In all the world who had the comprehension
To ask intelligent or clever questions,
And one of them was certainly not me.

"Now, long ago, there was a curious
New essence postulated to be found
Throughout the universe, and to surround
All objects that we see, ubiquitous,
But otherwise somewhat mysterious;
A quite unusual and strange compound
Transmitting light, but certainly not sound,
This *ether* thus was 'luminiferous'.
The great Lord Kelvin tried a definition:
It was a million times less dense than air,
Invisible, untouchable and strong,
Inert and frictionless, and in addition,
This medium for light was everywhere,
A speculation wonderful, but wrong."

While young, he made a thought-experiment:
Himself and mirrors, speeding fast as light,
And wondered if his facial image might
Be cancelled by the inconvenient
Prevention of escape of pertinent
Emissions, rays which then return as sight,
Assuming that their speed was fixed outright,
And passed through ether, (or its equivalent).
But other thinkers, back to Galileo,
Imagined similar and self-enclosed
Procedures, going at a lesser speed;
Observers there, inside, how could they know
What speed, if any such, had been imposed,
With smooth and constant motion guaranteed?

This first imagined system thus had need
Of fixed external points of reference,
In order that a traveler might sense
That he was going at a certain speed.
But Einstein's would allow him to proceed
Entirely circumscribed, the difference
Was at the speed of light, where evidence
Of motion would be obvious, indeed.
These two constructions formed a paradox
Not easily resolved, for each one made
Assumptions which the other one rejected.
For travelers inside the enclosed box,
Which theory more honestly portrayed
Realities which he himself detected?

In Galileo's relativity,
(All motions in an isolated space
Are relative to others in that place,
But not to outside reference), the key
Is where the one observing this might be;
Assuming this observer's constant base
To be inside the unit would erase
The influence of outside energy.
But if, as on a platform at a station,
One sees a train pass by, then all inside
Will seem (at uniform velocity)
To pass and disappear without relation
To smaller motions which might coincide
Within the train, without validity.

And similar to this was Einstein's dream,
But having one important variation,
The speed of light was constant in relation
To eyes of the observer; this might seem
Nonsensical at first, that such a beam
Would strike an eye, no matter its location
And let him see his face (its derivation)
Whether speed was low or was extreme.
Was Galileo wrong? Or did the light
Go through the ether at a shifting speed?
So, which was right? The answer here was "neither";
The speed of light was fixed and constant, quite
Related to his eye, it had no need
For mediums, there was no ether, either.

In nineteen-hundred-five, that was the year
That suddenly the "firestorm" struck his mind;
His thinking crystallized, his thoughts combined
And suddenly the universe was clear.
He analyzed the particles that veer
In jerky motions (Brownian), defined
As random movements of the unaligned
Free molecules and atoms moving here.
Extrapolating from this observation,
He argued that all matter was composed
Of particles like these, the molecules
And atoms, in a varied combination
Resulted in a system that was closed,
Dynamic, but contained by certain rules.

He also found a well-defined effect
(Photo-electric) which could be explained
By quantum physics, if (as Planck maintained)
The energy and heat that we detect
(Both radiated and absorbed) reflect
Small particles, discrete and unconstrained
By any need that they must be contained
Within the classic rules that we expect.
Until his era smooth, continuous
Absorption of a force or energy
By any solid mass, or its emission
By radiation from a nucleus
Seemed logical and clear, thus it should be
Accepted as the orthodox position.

But Einstein said the quantum theory
Applied to light itself, with tiny pieces
Or bits of energy the source releases,
Their strength depending on their frequency.
These particles (or *photons)* that we see
Control the brightness as their sum increases
(The light turned off, the stream of photons ceases),
And color by their innate energy.
Experiments had shown that light behaves
And has some features (such as frequency)
That led the physics world to analyze
Its nature as a constant line of waves.
But Einstein showed that particles must be
Involved somehow; for this he won a prize.

His work on *special* relativity
Was published, almost as an afterthought,
And contradicted things that had been taught
For centuries, until complacency
Induced a petrified and fixed decree
That left inquiring minds like his distraught,
Regarding possibilities which ought
To be evaluated carefully.
He dreamed of riding on a beam of light
When he was young; subliminal suggestion
Remained until maturity could give
A satisfactory account despite
The difficulty of this present question:
Was all the universe, then, relative?

Two lighted trains go racing through the night
On tracks adjacent, parallel and straight;
The darkness will surround and isolate
The two from any fixed external sight.
The other train provides the only light
By which to judge their pace, a steady state;
As long as one does not accelerate,
Their speed seems imperceptible or slight.
But then with dawn the outer world appears,
And moving in a retrograde direction
Gives evidence of great velocity.
This change of reference now interferes
With our illusion, forcing a rejection
Of what we had assumed so recently.

"Accept the fact," he said, "Though I could show
By complex mathematic formulae
That what my stories of the trains imply
Can be confirmed, but these you should forego.
It is sufficient now that you should know
The law that these examples clarify:
That speed observed by any passer-by
Depends upon his own, a ratio.
And since the speed of light can never change
(According to the Maxwell calculation),
With greater distance, time is magnified.
To human eyes and minds this shift is strange,
Too small and subtle for examination,
But it is real and can be verified."

"A resting state has zero time dilation,
But relative dynamics will reveal
A change in intervals, and these are real
But too minute for human observation.
This shift is true and not imagination;
Surprisingly it also has to deal
With size and space, perhaps it must repeal
Historic absolutes for *variation*."
To this remarkable scenario
(Though all his logic and equations fit)
Objections and uncertainty arose.
As Einstein said himself, "For all I know,
The Lord is laughing at me over it,
And leading me around as by the nose."

"For surely it would be ridiculous
To think that size and weight depend on speed,
And that one's point of view might somehow lead
To changes that were not fortuitous.
But mathematic proofs, while arduous,
Will force the greatest skeptics to concede
That even nonconformists may indeed
Engage in science that is rigorous."
And this is what he did, for subsequent
Experiments confirmed, in proper course,
His *special* work on relativity.
This concept, these equations represent
A radical departure from their source,
Which lay in Galileo's theory.

Not satisfied with "special" finite laws
(For objects moving at a constant speed),
He followed them to see where they might lead,
And was amazed at what he found, because
Applied to gravity they showed the flaws
In Newton's cosmic vision, and indeed
Produced a picture that was guaranteed
To earn respect and general applause.
He postulated space in four dimensions
(With three for space itself, and one for time),
Much like a stretchy fabric that could change
According to the various distentions
Created by the masses that may climb
Or fall, or cycle, orbit, rearrange.

A massive star will plunge into a space
Distorting it into a deep depression,
As if its energy and stark aggression
Required resistance for a resting place.
And lesser densities which interface
With greater suns that hold them in possession
Will circle, and will make their own impression
Upon the slope of fabric they embrace.
The even smaller moons, in one direction
In which they orbit planets they must follow,
Will carve their own concavities through space.
Their energy would tend to cause ejection
But counter-action keeps them in their hollow;
Thus gravity retains them in their place.

Opposing conflicts to this theorem
(Which he called *general* relativity)
Demanded proofs of great consistency
And rigor that no critic could condemn.
This was his way of calculating them:
He found potential energy (or "*e*")
Was equal to the speed of light (or "*c*")
If squared and times the mass involved (or "*m*").
A balance was maintained in every stratum
Of matter in the universe, each sun
Each planetary system, galaxy,
In every molecule, within each atom
And sub-atomic particle, each one
Contained immense but stable energy.

The work on relativity began
Within a single free imagination,
But rather than result in validation
Of Newton's principles and cosmic plan,
It stretched the limits and then over-ran
The well-defined reciprocal relation
Affecting gravity, its augmentation
With larger mass, decrease with greater span.
And yet the later work was built on this:
That time, both absolute and mathematic
Was independent of external things,
And flowed from its internal genesis
To govern processes which may be static
Or as dynamic as vibrating strings.

In other words, it passes constantly
The same for one in motion or at rest.
Events will happen, time will have progressed,
Its measurement a mere formality.
And so it was, until our century,
For all occasions in our sight suggest
That time cannot expand or be compressed,
And goes one way, as far as we can see.
Our lives proceed from *past* into the *present*,
And seem to be decisive as they pass;
A statement made can never be un-spoken,
No matter that results might be unpleasant;
We hold within our hands a fragile glass
Which if it breaks, remains forever broken.

A third of one millennium ago
There was another year, miraculous,
When Newton found the truly serious
Attractions that all objects undergo,
Each with all others, forces that will grow
With larger masses in a rigorous
Proportion; will, although ubiquitous,
Decrease with distance by an inverse ratio.
This law, of which he was the architect,
Seemed universal, final, and concrete.
But he remained uneasy, not because
His formulas and laws were incorrect,
But that, while true, they might be incomplete;
He was not certain that was all there was.

And Newton was, as usual, correct,
His work, while never *wrong* was incomplete;
The world that he inhabited was neat,
In three dimensions, simple, circumspect.
There, laws and mathematics intersect
To prove that fantasies are obsolete,
And that there are realities that meet
In finite time and space, where they connect.
His great <u>Principia,</u> the starting place,
The great divide between the old and new,
The first to satisfy our modern rules
For evidence regarding outer space,
Was only one beginning leading to
The laws that govern stars, and molecules.

He also was the last who could impose
His mathematics, formulas and laws
Upon the world of science, just because
It seemed that they completely would enclose
All possibilities; his only foes
Were somewhat jealous, yet they found no flaws.
But after Newton, harmony would pause
As scientific give-and-take arose.
Hypotheses then led reliably
To arguments and petty bickerings,
And controversy now is more extensive;
As studies increase geometrically
So many people know so many things,
But no one's knowledge now is comprehensive.

We like to think our world is always stable,
A solid base from which one can begin
To calculate a principle; but then,
Not long ago humanity was able
To credit and believe the ancient fable
(Erroneous, to everyone's chagrin,
And yet denied at risk of mortal sin),
That Earth was flat and shaped much like a table.
Then, though Columbus proved the world was round,
It still was thought to be the very center
Of all the universe; this was until
Copernicus and Galileo found
(Regardless of the Church, their great tormenter)
That we went round the sun, and it stood still.

And now, in place of these naïve delusions
Which seem so primitive in retrospect
(An insult to the human intellect),
We have a new assortment of confusions.
For quantum physics came to these conclusions:
That accidents that happen will connect
As time goes by, will lead us to expect
Uncertainty, misfortunes and illusions.
Then Kurt Gödel evolved his *incompleteness*
Which, added to *uncertainty* appears
To lead to *chaos* and a limitless
Descent into a state without concreteness.
Will we, on looking back in future years
Consider this our current foolishness?

The quantum theory was postulated
On sub-atomic particles in space
Existing in their single point or place
That time and energy had designated.
And though their cycles might be complicated,
The neutrons and the protons interlace
To form a nucleus on which to base
The orbits of electrons, separated.
And even empty space is filled with pairs
Of particles and anti-particles
The energy of which is infinite;
But since each unit of the two-some shares
Resistance to the other, each annuls
Effective movement of its opposite.

But what if basic objects are not *things*
Or *particles* that occupy locations?
Perhaps we build existence on *vibrations*
Produced by tiny lines called *superstrings*.
Within this model is a force that brings
Its webs, divisions and re-combinations,
With constant motion, waves and oscillations
Where particles are felt as quiverings.
But this is only speculation, since
There is no proof, not one experiment
To show that any superstring exists;
Proponents thus cannot as yet convince
The world that ten dimensions represent
The whole of which the universe consists.

And thus there are some questions still remaining:
Are there dimensions that we cannot see?
Beyond the four we know (in space are three,
In time is one); hypotheses containing
A greater number find that they are straining
The balance of the world, stability
Of all the universe, the harmony
Which now exists, requiring no explaining.
And some may ask why gravity is weak
Contrasted to electro-magnetism,
Are particles mere waves along a string?
And are we chasing a mirage to seek
With any realistic optimism,
A unified design of everything?

Perhaps there truly is an integration
Remaining to be found by someone wise
Who has the diligence to analyze
Conflicting theories of our creation;
And yet there may not be just one equation
But several that equally comprise
A sequence that will someday organize
A rational, accepted explanation.
But what if none of these is adequate?
Events might be completely arbitrary
Without a pattern we can recognize;
Some said (like Newton) God would not forget
But would in time provide a solitary
Solution He alone could synthesize.

No human ever is infallible,
And even those of genius make mistakes;
The intellect is flawless but forsakes
The one it serves, the highest pinnacle
Defeats the strongest and most powerful
Of mountain climbers, oxygen still makes
The body function, absence overtakes
The sharp perceptive mind and makes it dull.
Achievement on the highest plane of thought
Like mountaineering at the greatest height
Inspires and rouses, but the penalty
For error is severe; at least one ought
To be judicious lest an oversight
Or over-reaching cause catastrophe.

In Newton's era, heaven was a scene
Of perfect harmony, a metaphor
Of God's own flawless essence, and therefore
Eternal, everlasting and serene;
And he had faith that God would intervene
Whenever it was necessary for
Averting incidents He would abhor
That formed a danger to divine routine.
Regrettably, his plan of gravity
Predicted that the cosmos would collapse;
But he was honest in his own arena
And would not alter mathematics he
Had carefully constructed, but perhaps
He could rely on *"deus ex machina"*.

And so it was with Einstein, there are two
Examples of a flaw that even he
Could not predict, anticipate, foresee
And thus perhaps prevent: he could pursue
A concept that was radical but true,
And yet he longed for beauty, symmetry,
A balance without ambiguity
Contained within the old, and in the new.
And so he altered some of his equations
By introducing ill-defined techniques;
Extraneous, they did not quite belong,
And yet, with arguments and with evasions
He guarded them against adverse critiques
While secretly he knew that they were wrong.

Throughout his life he never had believed
In universal instability
Created by unbalanced energy,
The forces he himself had just conceived.
To equalize this power he retrieved
A "cosmic constant" from his memory,
Designed to balance stresses equally,
And validate the system he'd achieved.
This factor, later proven artificial
Was entered into his equations, fudged
In order to produce a certain state
Which he predicted prior to initial
Precise and careful proof; but he misjudged
The awkwardness that this would generate.

He studied this, admitted his mistake,
The "cosmologic constant" did not fit
With relativity, but altered it;
What was transparent then became opaque.
(When Friedmann built his models, he would make
The constant *zero*, basically omit
The factor altogether, *Infinite*
Became a path the universe might take.)
Although he made an effort to prolong
This artificial constant, somewhat later
The evidence began to make him wonder;
At last he recognized that he was wrong,
Apologized to Friedmann and Lemaitre,
Confessing that it was his greatest blunder.

Much later Einstein faced a quandary;
The quantum physics built by Planck and Bohr
Was anything but classic, and therefore
Conflicted with his relativity.
Beginnings may involve an agency
(Perhaps external) to arouse a core
To limitless expansions which ignore
Restrictions, and continue boundlessly.
But if the universe is self-contained,
The surface of both space and time is closed;
And this, together with *uncertainty*,
(A part of quantum physics) both maintained
Our universe would (always unopposed),
Not be created, but would simply *be*.

Throughout his later life he tried to find
A simple synthesis, a common ground
Between the relativity he found
And quantum particles, these two combined
Would certainly explain what lies behind
The energy and forces which surround
And move the universe; but all renowned
And brilliant men had failed, so did his mind.
The places he had gone had been unknown,
His name alone became a synonym
For intellect, but he could not deliver
A harmony of all that then was known;
He was like Moses, when God said to him,
"Go just this far, but do not cross the river."

In every life there comes a certain time
To look at all the things that have been done,
Considering the value of the prime
Unfactored essence of the work begun,
And what of this was finished? If complete
Is all the outcome still benevolent?
This summing up, a final balance-sheet
Defines the center of accomplishment.
And if the core, the body, is unique,
It should be cause to feel a certain pride;
If you discover things that all men seek,
The soul at closing should be satisfied.
But his was not, for always in his mind
The Ultimate remained still undefined.

"When young, I found the world a complex mess,
With mathematics, thought I found a sure
And proven path which truly could express
Eternal order, beautiful and pure.
But even after relativity,
Came work of Heisenberg and Kurt Gödel,
With incompleteness and uncertainty,
And we were once more on the carousel,
All whirling round a center still elusive
And reaching for a prize we could not touch.
But I believe, despite the inconclusive
Results of axioms and proofs and such,
Reality and truth exist out there,
The problem is that none of us know where."

ENLIGHTENMENT AND UNDERSTANDING

Return to the mentor

If he was right, and truth was to be found,
I knew that I myself had much to learn;
Not only could I hardly yet discern
Reality when it was all around,
But could not separate the proven, sound
And orderly assurance from the churn
Of premise and hypothesis to earn
The confidence that comes with solid ground.
And where is truth? Does it lie somehow hidden,
So that you come upon it suddenly,
And wonder why you never were aware
Of such a trophy? Or is it forbidden
To all but mystics, some divinity,
And could I find its essence anywhere?

And as I wandered through the morning air,
Considering the molecules therein
The inert gases and the oxygen,
I wondered how the minute forces there
That hold those particles in place compare
With cosmic energy, adrenaline
That moves the universe; and then,
The sunlight glittered on a distant chair.
I saw my mentor there, restrained and waiting,
And knew that he would never criticize
The partial understanding I'd achieved.
So I looked forward to communicating
Again with someone who might summarize
And make some sense of what I had received.

Indeed, at first he asked me to begin
At the beginning of my travels through
The centuries of early thinkers who
Defined our scientific discipline.
For scientists in fact they all had been;
Their reasoning was critical and true,
No matter that their instruments were few
And none were really sound or genuine.
The first used only thought and open sight,
Inducing answers from the slightest clues;
The stars they saw when they looked overhead
Appeared to be a roof upon the night.
My teacher listened to these brief reviews,
The best I could assemble, then he said:

"You are correct, these men, who (mainly Greek)
Had use of reason and of common senses
(Their vision mainly), had no false pretenses
Since all their methods (in their world unique)
Included honest inquiry, to seek
For truth, and then accept the consequences;
For if they found some vital differences
From prejudice, they trusted their technique.
And so the back-and-forth of thought went on
With constant re-evaluation when
Some new ability would give an edge;
Thus many facts, proposed and then withdrawn,
Then modified, might surface once again,
Respected, not considered sacrilege."

"What you have heard is but an overview,
Much work was done by others in between;
And some was brilliant, some was mere routine,
Conjectures might prove false, or might be true."
And so it was, for he already knew
Where I had been, what I had heard and seen;
The things he told me would not supervene,
But add completeness that was overdue.
I knew all this, for in our modern time,
The sureness of a hundred years ago
Had given way, and progress seemed to stall;
Uncertainty, itself a paradigm,
Had come from scientists I did not know,
And then, compulsively, he named them all.

The recitation of the elements
Beginning: "Antimony, Arsenic
Aluminum, Selenium" is quick,
An easy aid for our intelligence;
Not so these men and their accomplishments.
Although his style was far from histrionic,
The summary was not at all mnemonic,
So painfully, I memorized events.
A great amount had happened recently,
Not all of which would prove to be correct,
Pure mathematics carries the temptation
To over-emphasize formality;
And therefore I was glad, in retrospect,
He had not put their names in an equation.

As brevity is still the soul of wit,
He did not qualify in this regard;
His ancient history I could discard
Since I already had the benefit
Of what the sources could themselves transmit.
And even recent summaries were marred
By earnest doubts, and questions that were hard,
Requiring judgments that were exquisite.
But try he did, and after Einstein's era
He plunged into the chaos modern thought
Had added to the cauldron of opinions,
Part scientific thought but part chimera,
It argued with itself although it sought
Perfection as defined by Augustinians.

(St. Augustine, though not a scientist,
Believed in progress toward an excellence
That would, in time, result with confidence
In perfect harmony, and co-exist
With man's pursuit of knowledge; so the list
Of schemes, conjectures, plans and arguments
Brought forth with (more or less) intelligence
Would blend, and satisfy each analyst.
And therefore all the current controversy
Was truly not outright antagonistic,
But each a part of general endeavor;
And man's resourcefulness, with God's own mercy,
Combined into a single altruistic
Conclusion that would dominate forever).

"A century ago it first was shown
That out in space, among the junk and rubble
(That telescopes could see without much trouble),
Were other stellar systems like our own.
All these were organized and fully-grown,
Facsimiles of ours, much like a double;
This finding frightened some when Edwin Hubble
Confirmed our galaxy was not alone.
In fact, he had discovered many others,
Which scattered over tracts of empty space
Appeared as in a spectrum, dim to bright,
The radiance of some much like another's.
But there were contrasts that he could retrace,
With most it was the color of their light."

85

"For some were red, but some a deeper red
(All shifted like all others, none towards blue);
From their intensity and from their hue
It could be calculated that they sped
Away from us, expanding overhead
Into an open universe, which grew
In ways that even Einstein never knew,
(For in this one respect he was misled).
But even more than this was rearranged,
For in the classic era Ptolemy
(Who followed Aristotle) had believed
The earth to be the center; this was changed
By Galileo, whose apostasy
Was largely true, but was not well-received."

"But Galileo was himself misled
To think our solar system was the core
Of all the universe and thus ignore
The many galaxies spread overhead.
Copernicus, before him, thought instead
The cosmos to be boundless, furthermore
There was no solid ceiling, wall or floor
The realm of Heaven was discredited.
But did this firmament expand with time?
Or did the stars remain in place and static,
Or possibly increase and then contract,
A massive, vast celestial pantomime?
For centuries, no one could be dogmatic,
But after Newton, things were more exact."

"For Newton, with his laws of gravity
Had indicated: masses would attract
All other masses (other stars in fact)
According to their size and weight; debris
Would fly into a star which then would be
Fair game for larger stars, and re-enact
This sequence that would tend to counteract
Prolonged expansion or stability.
His mathematics seemed to indicate
That stars and galaxies move toward each other
Until they meet at some essential site,
And all the heavens fall and concentrate,
Thus canceling the motion of each other;
The world would then become eternal night."

"But if the galaxies were infinite,
And scattered uniformly (more or less)
Through space that in itself did not possess
A limit or an edge, each star would fit
Into a random placement, and would sit
Distributed through equal emptiness;
Without a central focus, no access
To gravity is possible for it.
The universe would endlessly stay static
With each component fixed into its spot,
And each itself a solitary center.
Infinity is therefore problematic,
With difficulties Einstein saw (somewhat),
But could not solve." And neither could my mentor.

But he went on, reviewing history,
As if to bring my knowledge of the past
Into the present time and to contrast
Its fantasies with our reality.
"Before our current era *heresy*
(A term applied to an iconoclast)
Inhibited research that might forecast
Alternatives to sound theology.
So *heaven,* also *hell,* must both be placed
Within the cosmos, which must be created
By God Himself at one specific time.
And any observation which displaced
Accepted orthodoxy deviated
From *truth revealed,* and was itself a crime."

"Then Hubble reckoned distances to nine
Of all the millions of the galaxies,
And proved that earlier hypotheses
Must be corrected, or must re-align,
Resolve or modify, or re-define,
Adjusting to the new realities;
With counsel from a modern Socrates
Perhaps the old and new could both combine.
A star's inherent luminosity
Can indicate a change in its location,
And every galaxy that Hubble scanned
Had color-shifts enough to guarantee
A rapid retrograde acceleration;
The universe was proven to expand."

"This finding that the stars were in transition
And never are considered to be static
Would violate the previous dogmatic
Religious doctrines, which by intuition
Assumed creation, by its definition
Occurring once, was fixed and not erratic;
And on this point they all were quite emphatic:
That God created all by His volition.
And now this new expanding firmament
Disturbed conventional theology
And caused a great devotional confusion.
But there were others who were confident,
For Aristotle's Greek philosophy
Opposed the prospect of divine intrusion."

"Just *how* did all these fleeing stars begin?
Where at the end of time will they reside?
Will any of them veer and then collide?
Who turned them on, *what* was their origin?
These questions all arose with genuine
Anxiety in all on every side;
Some were concerned how science was applied,
And some with heresy and mortal sin.
A first initial cause (some said 'creator'),
Traditional among religious sects,
Was threatened by these new discoveries.
Some *one* or *thing* had been the activator
Of violent celestial effects
But which it was defied analyses."

"Since all the stars are moving rapidly
Away from us, the universe, expanding,
Must once have been much smaller, notwithstanding
That none of us on earth, unaided, see
A difference from year to year; the key
Is total time elapsed, the course demanding
A thousand million years before the landing
Of light upon the earth from nebulae.
But granting this immense amount of time,
The motion of the stars in retrograde
Would indicate that somewhere out in space
At one unique split-second, at the prime
Event in history the stars' cascade
Began exactly from a single place."

"Before this moment, time did not exist,
The universe was infinitely small
And motion was suspended there for all;
There was no force, and nothing to resist,
Until an overall protagonist
Arose and summoned up a critical
Intensity that would be integral
And serve as all-inclusive catalyst.
Thus all that was to follow started there,
When stars were scattered into empty space
And time had its beginning with a bang;
Then matter seemed to travel everywhere
And fleeing galaxies were commonplace,
But ultimately, would they boomerang?"

"What was the energy that was imparted?
We know from Newton's work on gravity,
A strong attraction will accompany
Two masses just as soon as they are parted.
Regardless of the distance they have darted
There still will be a force that constantly
Attempts to re-unite them and will be
Incentive to return to where they started.
And so a power that strives to separate
A unity and scatter all its sections
Must counteract and even must surpass
(If it itself is to accelerate)
This counterforce which acts in all directions
And seeks to re-create a single mass."

"If gravity predominates (is greater
Than its antagonist), circumference
Along with each dimension will condense;
The galaxy will involute, and later
Collapse into itself, a cosmic crater.
This would result in one immensely dense
And compact mass, which being so intense,
May cancel both itself and its creator.
But if within a galaxy the forces
Which separate the stars and send them flying
Are larger than the powers of attraction,
The entity expands, as do the courses
Of all the suns within, thus amplifying
Their orbits, an unbalanced counter-action."

"Thus, if a universe survives at rest,
Offsetting of these forces is essential;
For if there is a crucial differential
With energy on either side expressed
And unopposed, the outcome is at best
A very large unbalancing potential,
And at the worst a crisis, exponential;
Cascading change will soon be manifest.
Because of this, a static universe
Was so important Einstein added on
A 'cosmic constant' to his theory,
An 'anti-gravity' that would disperse
These forces evenly, both pro-and-con,
And rectify his relativity."

"But Alexander Friedmann soon corrected
This error (that the universe was static),
The theories of Einstein were emphatic
And relativity itself projected
Expansion of the universe, detected
Diffusely everywhere, a systematic
Enlargement that was not at all erratic,
But could, by anyone, have been expected.
The Friedmann model (that the universe
Appears identical in each direction
If it is viewed on an enormous scale),
Was proven later; galaxies disperse
Away from one another, their connection
Progressively more delicate and frail."

"The universe is like a large balloon,
Each distal galaxy a painted spot.
And as the globe grows larger, they are not
Unchanged or stationary or immune
To stretching and distension; they are soon
Across the sky, and burning fiery hot,
But each more isolated like the dot
Which, with expansion, is more widely strewn.
Diameters increase, the spots or stars
Will move apart much faster now that they
Are on the surface of a larger sphere.
But still one thing in these particulars,
Among this multitude, this vast array,
No single one will be the center here."

"The Friedmann models raised three alternates,
And each of them depended on the speed
With which expansion promised to exceed
The force of gravity, which operates
A stable circling system that awaits
Another power willing to concede
An equal balance, this a prize indeed:
That neither of the forces dominates.
But it is likely that the universe
May follow its expansion to the end,
Through forces stronger than its gravity
And then extend forever and disperse
To spaces that we cannot comprehend
But wish, like Moses, we could only see."

"A universe that grows too leisurely
Might find that gravitational attraction
Between the many galaxies in action
Would cause its growth to slow to some degree,
And then to stop; reversing energy
Would bring about an overall contraction
Until its total volume is a fraction,
Decreasing with a great velocity.
The distances between the stars decline
To end at zero, where they once began;
The correlation is that density
(Reciprocal to size) will re-align,
Increasing with each stage of smaller span,
And ultimately reach infinity."

"There still is one more option possible,
In which a kind of equilibrium
Has been achieved, the force is medium,
Enough to create all the miracle
Of universal birth, but not annul
The binding gravity, which will become
A stabilizing stress with maximum
Effect, no nadir and no pinnacle.
Which model best describes our universe?
The answer cannot now be absolute.
Uncertainty is great, not only *distance*
But *matter* which we cannot see, and worse,
Which may have gravity and constitute
A threat to universal co-existence."

"Yet all the models Friedmann had defined
(No matter what the outcome) had one thing
In common to them all, a happening
A thousand million years ago, designed
By some as yet obscure and hidden mind.
The cosmos, miniscule to vanishing
Had weight and compactness embodying
The mass of all the galaxies combined;
With radius of zero, density
And curve of space and time were infinite.
As general relativity predicted
The entire universe was seemingly
Condensed into a single point, and it
Was dormant, inert, motionless, restricted."

"At some as yet unknown and arbitrary
And random place in time, a singular
Event occurred; each galaxy and star
Broke free in one supreme extraordinary
Discharge of energy, from sedentary
To being in one moment flung to far
Arenas of the universe. They are
Still there, still circling, still incendiary.
And this unique result, though imprecise,
Has been described as one enormous bang,
Occurring once, dividing history,
Postponing tranquil peace and paradise
In favor of chaotic worlds, which sprang
From one encounter with our destiny."

"For centuries, this led to great contention;
The Greeks were not enamored of creation
Or of its mirror-image, liquidation.
And Aristotle looked on intervention
(Divine or otherwise) with condescension;
For life was surely stable, alteration
Was not permitted, no supreme causation
Could change the world in even one dimension.
The monotheists (Christians, Muslims, Jews)
Believed there was a prime initial cause
Explaining how the universe began,
But had a problem when they had to choose
A date for this divine event, the laws
Diverged for Scripture, science and Koran."

"Then Augustine, much braver than the rest,
Suggested: 'Seven thousand years ago.'
The book of Genesis led him to know
Of all the options, this one date was best.
When Hubble had the data to suggest
That Augustine's result was far too low
It forced theology to undergo
Revision of the doctrines it professed.
Like Galileo's concept of the sun
The Church rejected all these observations;
At first it threatened heresy and libel,
Until at last in nineteen fifty one
The Pope admitted that these calculations
Could be correct according to the Bible."

"If it is true that all of time began
When energy and substance, both combined
In one immense explosion, re-aligned
The universe into its present span
(A volume now immense, gargantuan,
And still expanding, not to be confined),
How could we know what eras lay behind?
(For prior time was not within this plan).
We do not know what caused this great beginning,
A physical necessity, or God,
(Perhaps He acted at a later time,
But was most certainly the underpinning,
As if He searched with a divining rod
For some improved and newer paradigm)."

"We look across the heavens in an arc;
The stars and galaxies are specks of light
Illuminated through the blackest night
As if each one contains a vital spark.
But in between are spaces that are dark,
Congested matter hidden to our sight,
The opposite of that which seems so bright,
But which in secret still can make its mark.
Dark matter often takes another shape;
Black holes that scattered through the universe
Have gravity so strong it sucks one in,
Not even letting light itself escape,
Like theologic doctrine with its curse
Of children who are damned by primal sin."

"So time is also finite in extent,
But like a line that has two boundaries:
Where it begins, and what no person sees,
An ending which is not an accident.
Each one of us can look at different
Experiences in our past but these
Cannot be carried forward, destinies
Are there, but veiled, to our bewilderment.
Is there, for *time*, an absolute beginning?
Or does it cycle in a steady state,
As gravity induces *space* to bend.
Go travel on the earth (while it is spinning),
In one straight line, and you anticipate
A journey in a circle, with no end."

"The answers still are not entirely clear,
But we may ask the questions, (time and space,
Since both are altered by their interface
With gravity, may bend and thus appear
To have no boundary and no frontier):
Will bending round upon themselves erase
Infinity? Is there a resting place,
Or will continued motion interfere?
And how are energy and mass related?
Since Einstein proved by his well-known equation
That changes in the one affect the other,
The consequence is endlessly debated
Concerning outcomes of this correlation,
And will it change our world into another?"

"It once was possible, in Newton's day
To understand the whole enlightenment
That humans had achieved; intelligent
And educated people felt that they
Could understand, compare, at least survey
The implications of each new event.
Their grasp of all of life was prominent
And 'Renaissance' in knowledge no cliché.
But since that time, there has been such a pace
Of major findings, so accelerated
That *insight* is impaired (and convoluted
Discoveries uncertain); in their place,
As soon as one result was indicated
It might by other studies be refuted."

"In recent years, contrasting theories
Have been proposed, describing other ways
The universe might reach its present phase,
How matter and opposing energies
Could interact, and all the galaxies
Conform to laws which each of them obeys
Without the "bang", or forceful breakaways
That hurled them out at high velocities.
One postulate was called the "steady state,"
But this involved continuous creation,
Of matter that would fill and reconcile
Expanding space that it would permeate.
It was abandoned after refutation
By Penzias and Wilson, and by Ryle."

"Another rival to the singular
Beginning of the universe (intense,
Unique in time and space, with violence
Creating every galaxy and star),
Was one in which the macrocosms are
Sequential, they expand and then condense,
Their particles contract and then commence
A second balanced mode, still circular.
Two Russians, Lifshitz and Khalatnikov
Proposed this plan which was a give-and-take,
A universe that falls, then escalates.
It traced the Einstein-Friedmann model of
The cosmos, but was proven a mistake
By Roger Penrose and associates."

"Sir Arthur Eddington believed that he
(With Einstein, too) alone could comprehend
A new and novel plan which would extend
The absolutes of Newton's gravity.
Revision of the role of *energy*
Affecting *mass*, and which could warp and bend
Both space and time would therefore now transcend
The stable basis of theology.
But that was over eighty years ago,
Now tens of thousands fully understand
(And millions more at least can recognize)
The core of relativity, although
Not one of us is able to command
The insight which will be the final prize."

And then he said: "There is much more to teach
Had I the time, and you the tolerance.
But physics covers such a wide expanse
That things already are beyond your reach,
And past the ones who think and those who preach,
Philosophers confused by circumstance
And prophets with decreasing relevance,
A synthesis beyond the grasp of each.
But scientists are equally to blame
For asking *what* and *how* but never *why*.
If there is still a place for God the Father,
Responsible for what the world became
And for the universe, the stars and sky,
For earth and for our lives, why did He bother?"

"The imperfections and complexity
Of His creation and of all therein
Would disillusion even genuine
Celestial forces working properly.
So is our world an inconsistency,
An accident (to heavenly chagrin),
Escaping His intended discipline,
Or some divine and sacred comedy?
If we, an afterthought, a codicil,
Are ever to become God's standard-bearer,
His total process of creation might
Be sentenced to repeat itself until
(Through countless episodes of trial and error)
Creator or created gets it right."

"So quantum physics may indeed prevail,
Replacing classic relativity.
Its concept of disorder, *entropy*
Can create chaos on a larger scale
As time goes by; it also can derail
Chronology which travels normally
From past to present to what is to be,
(And might someday reverse our fairy-tale).
We look into the future, which is veiled,
From lives that are exhausted and outworn,
We seek eternal bliss until at last
Our struggle with the mind of God has failed.
As boats against the current, we are borne
Against our will again into the past."

"And still we search for one great unified
Design which might conform to everything.
But if we find it, will it coincide
With God, His will, and our imagining?
For Einstein posed the question: 'Is there need
For a Creator? Did He have a role
In choosing the conditions, or concede,
His only place was in the human soul?
Or did He breathe His fire into equations
And make a universe they could define,
The most compatible of all creations
With which our human entities align?' "
And having told me all that he could say
With grace and some regret he went away.

But now I knew, or only thought I knew
The laws that governed all the universe,
The energy that, seeking to disperse
The galaxies, antagonistic to
The force of gravity which always drew
All masses back together, these rehearse
The future of the stars that intersperse
With matter that is darkened to our view.
The vast preponderance of mass is dark,
As are our lives; we try but are unable
To find familiar bearings or to see
Which way to go, or where we should embark.
And all the things that we had thought were stable
Are whirling with a great velocity.

And if a speed becomes a higher speed
(As atoms subject to acceleration),
It is accepted that the correlation
Of energy and mass will always lead
To changes in the mass itself, indeed
An increase in its weight; this illustration
Has shown that principles of conservation
Of matter and of energy agreed.
But with increase in weight we ought to see
Some changes in the mutual attraction
Of all the other particles that must
By Newton's law stay balanced (gravity
Is modified by energetic action);
With any change, they all must re-adjust.

But balance is dynamic, never static,
And every motion has its counteraction;
Expansion is inherent with contraction
And both together make a systematic
Order, which is constant, not erratic.
Within the larger whole, each smaller fraction
Obeys the law of mutual attraction,
The system is symmetric and pragmatic.
This law is also true for us; each breath
Drawn in must be exhaled before a new
Succession can begin, and thus aeration
Maintains our vital life. And so is death,
The shadow of our lives, a pathway to
Renewal and continuous creation.

As darkness is essential for the light
To demonstrate its essence, all who live
Must also die. There is no positive
Without an equal negative, the night
Must balance opposite to daytime's bright
And often blinding sun; so relative
Antagonists provide a way to give
Disparate factors pathways to unite.
And motion, also having limitation
Cannot continue to infinity
Without renewing energy; with dual
Importance of exhaustion and creation
It must, preserving its stability,
Achieve a resting state before renewal.

And like the basic filaments that lose
Their energy through time, fatigue and stress,
So too the vigor that we all possess
When young, with age will fade and then diffuse
Into a weakened state; nor can we use
Our prayers or magic dreams or effortless
Petitions now. Our strength will still regress
And leave us with a single path to choose.
The only power we still retain must now
Surrender for a greater bliss, release
From earth where only mortal feet have trod
To heaven where immortals fly, allow
The spirit to accept and find its peace
Within the pure eternal heart of God.

The wheel has come full circle, here we are,
All facing once again into the center.
Somehow, no matter how we stray afar,
Regardless of whatever space we enter,
We are not whole ourselves, and what we lack
Will frighten and distress us, so that soon
A great compelling force will call us back,
As gravity controls a circling moon.
The memories of love to those alone
Call "re-unite" no matter what the cost.
To neutralize the fear of that unknown,
Illuminate the darkness of the lost,
A single image will command our sight
As does a beacon through chaotic night.

And here, where it began, will also end
The restless constant motion and the force
That once impelled a universe to send
Itself to unknown limits from its source.
So all remains in balance, still the laws
Of gravity and motion stay intact,
The greatest plan of all will merely pause
Before beginning once again to act.
And re-enaction will again transcend
All limitations and imagined flaws,
For human minds can never comprehend
The will of God that is the primal cause,
And sends to us His love, from whence derives
The universe, the stars, and all our lives.

End of Part I of "*Sacred Verses*"